English Workbook

Grammar and Punctuation

AGE 9–11

Susan Elkin

GALORE PARK
AN HACHETTE UK COMPANY

About the author

Susan Elkin is an award-winning journalist who has taught English in five different secondary schools, both independent and state, over many years, most recently at Benenden. She is the author of over 30 books including *English Year 9* and the *English A* Study Guide* and has been a regular contributor to many newspapers and magazines including the *Daily Telegraph* and *Daily Mail*. She is Education Editor at *The Stage* and writes blogs for *The Independent*. You can read about Susan's early classroom experiences in her 2013 ebook *Please Miss We're Boys*.

Every effort has been made to trace all copyright holders, but if any have been inadvertently overlooked the publishers will be pleased to make the necessary arrangements at the first opportunity.

Although every effort has been made to ensure that website addresses are correct at time of going to press, Galore Park cannot be held responsible for the content of any website mentioned in this book. It is sometimes possible to find a relocated web page by typing in the address of the home page for a website in the URL window of your browser.

Hachette UK's policy is to use papers that are natural, renewable and recyclable products and made from wood grown in well-managed forests and other controlled sources. The logging and manufacturing processes are expected to conform to the environmental regulations of the country of origin.

Orders: please contact Hachette UK Distribution, Hely Hutchinson Centre, Milton Road, Didcot, Oxfordshire, OX11 7HH. Telephone: (44) 01235 400555. Email: primary@hachette.co.uk. Lines are open from 9 a.m. to 5 p.m., Monday to Friday.

Parents, Tutors please call: 020 3122 6405 (Monday to Friday, 9:30 a.m. to 4.30 p.m.).

Email: parentenquiries@galorepark.co.uk

Visit our website at www.galorepark.co.uk for details of revision guides for Common Entrance, examination papers and Galore Park publications.

First published in 2014 by Galore Park Publishing Limited
Hodder & Stoughton Limited
An Hachette Company
Carmelite House
50 Victoria Embankment
London EC4Y 0DZ
www.galorepark.co.uk

Text copyright © Susan Elkin Ltd. 2014
The right of Susan Elkin to be identified as the author of this Work has been asserted by her in accordance with sections 77 and 78 of the Copyright, Designs and Patents Act 1988.

Impression number 15 14 13 12 11 10 9 8
Year 2025 2024 2023 2022 2021

All rights reserved. No part of this publication may be sold, reproduced, stored in a retrieval system, or transmitted, in any form or by any means, electronic, mechanical, photocopying, recording, or otherwise, without either the prior written permission of the copyright owner or a licence permitting restricted copying issued by the Copyright Licensing Agency, www.cla.co.uk

Typeset in India
Printed in India

A catalogue record for this title is available from the British Library.

ISBN: 978 1 471829 66 6

Contents

Introduction	4
Conjunctions	5
Nouns	8
Verbs	10
Adjectives	12
Adverbs	14
What exactly is a sentence?	16
Changing the word order	18
Commas for lists	20
Semicolons for lists	22
Collective nouns	24
Verb tenses	26
Compound nouns	28
Abstract nouns	30
Colons	32
Gerunds	33
Prepositions	34
Speech marks	36
Apostrophes for omission	38
Parenthesis	40
Apostrophes for possession	42
Fun with phrasal verbs	44
Flexible words	47
Adjectives with hyphens	50
Transitive verbs	52
Punctuation practice	54
Answers (pull-out middle section)	A1

Introduction

This workbook consists of 25 activities to help you understand grammar and punctuation better. Practice does indeed make perfect and these activities will help to further your understanding and provide plenty of opportunity to practise.

Using this book will help you to:

- recognise and use standard punctuation and grammar terminology
- punctuate your writing accurately so that the meaning is clear
- understand that precise punctuation is essential for effective communication
- manage the conventions of English grammar in your writing
- make sense of text by noticing ways in which grammar conveys and/or adds to meaning
- recognise links between punctuation and grammar.

So, who should use this book? It is intended for children at home working independently or with parents and for teachers in schools needing class work or homework tasks to consolidate learning. It could also be used as a revision book before exams.

Although this book is not linked to a particular examination syllabus it will help users prepare for the grammar and punctuation requirements of:

- Common Entrance 11+ in English
- 11+ entry English tests set by individual independent schools
- 11+ in English for selective state-funded schools in certain local authorities (such as Kent)
- National Curriculum Key Stage 2 SATs English tests
- pre-tests.

Where appropriate I have supplied sample answers in a pull-out section in the middle of the book. In this sort of work, however, there are often no specific right or wrong answers as the child is asked to think of his or her own examples.

Susan Elkin, September 2014

Conjunctions

A conjunction is a word such as 'and' or 'but' that joins sentences or parts of sentences to form one longer sentence.

For example:

> We live in Dulwich. There is no railway station.
>
> We live in Dulwich **and** there is no railway station.
>
> I like broccoli. My brother hates it.
>
> I like broccoli **but** my brother hates it.

Other conjunctions include because, whereas, since, although, unless, or, for, yet and so.

Three things to note and learn:

- Some of these words sometimes also do other jobs in sentences.
- It isn't strictly correct grammar (usually) to begin a sentence with a conjunction but we do it all the time in spoken English and, increasingly, in informal written English.
- You can change the underlying meaning, slightly or significantly, of a sentence by choosing a different conjunction.

> A *conjunction* is a joining word. Remember that a junction (such as Clapham Junction) joins railway lines.

Exercise

Underline the conjunctions in the sentences on the next two pages.

Then change each of the conjunctions to a different one. This may alter the meaning of the sentence.

Note briefly in brackets after each sentence what it now means.

For example:

> We go by rail to Scotland <u>unless</u> we need a car there.
>
> We go by rail to Scotland **although** we need a car there. (*We need a car in Scotland so we might have to hire one.*)

1 You should eat green vegetables so you'll be healthy.

_____

_____

_____

_____ (3)

2 She worked hard although she was badly paid.

_____

_____

_____

_____ (3)

3 In Britain you have to be 17 to drive a car whereas in parts of America you can start at 15.

_____

_____

_____

_____ (3)

4 He says he dislikes reading yet he does a lot of it.

_____

_____

_____

_____ (3)

5 Please visit us and we'll show you the local sights.

_____

_____

_____

_____ (3)

6 Ask and you will receive.

_____

_____

_____

_____ (3)

Conjunctions

7 I like all the swimming instructors at the club but Mr Jackson is my favourite.
_____
_____
_____
_____ (3)

8 Come over here so you can see the view from this window.
_____
_____
_____
_____ (3)

9 I shall choose a book by Michael Morpurgo or Theresa Breslin.
_____
_____
_____
_____ (3)

10 'Sit down and listen,' Mrs Summers or Mrs Erskine would say to us.
_____
_____
_____
_____ (3)

> Take note. Use short sentences with confidence. End them with full stops. Interspersed with longer, more complex sentences, they are a sign of good writing.

Nouns

A noun is a naming word.

Nouns name:
- objects (table, book)
- people (Queen Elizabeth, Michael Morpurgo)
- feelings (thirst, sadness)
- ideas (belief, racism).

Common nouns name objects (pencil, shoe).

Proper nouns name people (Emma Smith, Mrs Jones) and need capital letters.

Abstract nouns name feelings, ideas and conditions that you can't see or touch (determination, illness).

Collective nouns name groups of other nouns (pack of cards, flock of sheep).

Most common, abstract and collective nouns can be either singular (house, emotion, herd) or plural (houses, emotions, herds).

Words from Latin ending -us should really have an -i ending when they're plural: cacti, fungi, termini. It is quickly becoming acceptable, however, to use -es if you prefer. Language changes!

Most poetry uses a capital letter at the beginning of each line even when the word isn't a proper noun or the line isn't the beginning of a sentence.

Exercise

Underline all of the nouns in these sentences. Underneath each sentence write whether the nouns you've underlined are common, proper, abstract or collective.

1 Girls and boys usually like learning history.
   _____ (2)

2 On the way to Weymouth, Uncle Jake and I saw a lark and a charm of goldfinches.
   _____ (2)

3 Brighton and Eastbourne are towns on the south coast of England.
   _____ (2)

4 Mrs Peters spoke to each player in the team.
   _____ (2)

5 Guy Fawkes was found guilty of treason.
   _____ (2)

6 Maria Jensen has a passion for classical music.
   _____ (2)

7 Theft is illegal in every culture.
   _____ (2)

8 Questions and answers are welcome in all our lessons.
   _____ (2)

9 Did Jane Austen live in Hampshire?
   _____ (2)

10 Buckingham Palace is the main place of residence of Her Majesty the Queen.
   _____ (2)

Fun is a noun. 'We had fun at the school fête.' 'It is fun to run.' It really should not be used as an adjective ('We had a fun time at the school fête'). Try to find alternative adjectives such as *enjoyable, jolly, pleasant* or *cheerful*.

Verbs

A verb is an 'action' or 'being' word. It tells you what someone or something is doing, thinking or feeling, or what is happening. Verbs are the lifeblood of any language.

> The postman **arrived**.
>
> **Seen** this?
>
> I **thought** so.
>
> It **moved**.
>
> He **is** tired.

Data, criteria and media are plural nouns so they need plural verbs. (The media are [not 'is'] being regulated.)

Exercise 1

How many verbs can you think of which mean roughly the same as:

1 ran

_____
_____
_____ (5)

2 asked

_____
_____
_____ (5)

3 sat

_____
_____
_____ (5)

Exercise 2

Rewrite these sentences using your own choice of verbs in the gaps. Be as imaginative as you wish. Create at least two versions of each sentence.

1 Eva _____ while Bella _____ and George _____ . (1)

_____

_____

_____ (1)

2 Have you _____ ? (1)

_____

_____

_____ (1)

3 The mountain _____ as we _____ towards it. (1)

_____

_____

_____ (1)

4 I _____ hungry but my brother _____ not. (1)

_____

_____

_____ (1)

5 _____ while I _____ you how to do it. (1)

_____

_____

_____ (1)

6 Iris _____ much taller than Myrtle who _____ two years older. (1)

_____

_____

_____ (1)

11

Adjectives

The usual job of an adjective is to tell you more about a noun. In grammar we say that an adjective modifies or qualifies a noun.

> **black** cat
>
> **deep** hole
>
> **old** man
>
> **kind** Mr Ellerby
>
> **enormous** crowd of people
>
> **excellent** work

Along with other words that can change the meaning of another word, adjectives are sometimes called modifiers.

Some adjectives come from proper nouns. They are known as proper adjectives and need a capital letter.

> **Welsh** cheese
>
> **Shakespearean** verse
>
> **London** train

Exercise 1

Write twenty proper adjectives. Make them as varied as you can. Think of adjectives relating to people and places. Note that these words often end in **-ish** or **-ian**, although there are no rules.

Exercise 2

Underline the adjectives in these sentences. Underneath each sentence write different adjectives of your own choosing that would work as substitutes, changing the meaning of the sentence if you wish.

1 Most cattle in Britain are black and white or brown.
   _____ (2)

2 I shall ask helpful Mrs Smith or sarcastic Mr Fletcher.
   _____ (2)

3 Shall we go to the shopping centre or the local shops?
   _____ (2)

4 My father is a Newcastle boy but my mother is Liverpudlian.
   _____ (2)

5 You are late.
   _____ (2)

6 Italian cooking beats English or German offerings.
   _____ (2)

7 The centenarian grandmother was alert.
   _____ (2)

8 Good manners make happy teachers.
   _____ (2)

Station is a noun. It means a stopping place. It is therefore grammatically incorrect to refer to a *station stop* as many rail company staff do.

Adverbs

Adverbs do for verbs and adjectives what adjectives do for nouns. They modify, qualify or tell you more about them. Most adverbs answer one of these questions:

- How?
- When?
- Where?
- Why?

> He swam **strongly**.
>
> We waited **patiently**.
>
> **Silently**, I hoped.
>
> We **often** visited.
>
> He was an **outstandingly** fine player.

Many adverbs are formed by adding **-ly** to an adjective. Sometimes a slight adjustment in spelling is also needed.

> quick   quickly
>
> helpful   helpfully
>
> happy   happily

Other adverbs are independent words.

> seldom (They seldom went to church.)
>
> yet (Have you finished yet?)
>
> away (He went away.)

Exercise

1 Choose adverbs to put in the spaces in these sentences.

(a) Shall we leave _____ and drive _____ to the concert? (2)

(b) My grandfather is _____ good at Scrabble. (1)

(c) The family next door _____ goes for _____ long walks in the country. (2)

(d) Jocasta runs _____ and Noah _____ overtakes her. (2)

(e) 'It will _____ be time for bed' said Mum, _____. (2)

(f) My brother is _____ late for school although Dad _____ drops him off on time. (2)

(g) Do we _____ need to take all that gear with us? (1)

(h) Listen _____ and I'll explain _____ what we're going to do. (2)

2 Write five sentences using adverbs. Underline the adverbs in your work.

(a) _____ (2)

(b) _____ (2)

(c) _____ (2)

(d) _____ (2)

(e) _____ (2)

What exactly is a sentence?

A sentence is a group of words that makes sense on its own.

It must have a verb – an action or being word.

It begins with a capital letter.

It ends with a full stop (.) – which could be part of a question mark (?) or exclamation mark (!).

It can be very short.

Think of a sentence as a closed box, sealed by its capital letter at the beginning and full stop at the end.

Here are some examples of short simple sentences with the verbs in bold:

> Sophie **laughed**.
>
> **Has** Jack **arrived**?
>
> Hassan **is** here!

Within the box you may, if you wish, lengthen the sentence by adding other words separated by commas, which are weaker than full stops.

For example:

> Sophie, who is in Mrs Boyce's class, laughed.
>
> Has Jack, that boy from up the road, arrived yet?
>
> Hassan, my best friend's cousin, is here!

Notice that these commas work in pairs inside the sentence as if they were brackets. (See also page 40.)

> Do not use exclamation marks in your writing very often. Too many exclamation marks tend to make writing look weak. If what you say is well expressed you rarely need an exclamation mark to emphasise it.

Exercise

Now rewrite these sentences, adding to each some extra information enclosed in a pair of commas.

Don't forget to seal your sentences carefully with a clear capital letter at the beginning and a full stop (or question mark) at the end.

1 Did Ollie agree?
_____ (2)

2 Chloe cried.
_____ (2)

3 The school is closed.
_____ (2)

4 Jamila might know.
_____
_____ (2)

5 My train is late.
_____
_____ (2)

6 Has Panjit read it?
_____
_____ (2)

7 Even Tola liked it.
_____
_____ (2)

8 Felix stood up.
_____
_____ (2)

9 Wait for Emily.
_____
_____ (2)

10 Water is plentiful.
_____
_____ (2)

Changing the word order

Sometimes you can change the order of the words in a sentence without changing the meaning.

For example:

> Has Jack, that boy from up the road, arrived yet?
>
> Has that boy from up the road, Jack, arrived yet?
>
> Hassan, my best friend's cousin, is here!
>
> My best friend's cousin, Hassan, is here.

Sometimes it is necessary to add a few extra words.

For example:

> Sophie, who is in Mrs Boyd's class, laughed.
>
> A pupil in Mrs Boyd's class, Sophie, laughed.

> 'Me' is never the subject of a sentence – it's always 'I'. So it's: David and I went to town. If this puzzles you think what you'd say if the other person weren't involved. You'd say or write: I went to town.

Exercise

Look back at the sentences you built on page 17. Now write your ten sentences again on the opposite page, changing the order of the words without altering the meaning.

Experiment with this, but you will usually find that the extra words will sit well at the beginning of the sentence. You may find that this time you need a single comma rather than a pair, and you may find that you need to add some extra words.

Changing the word order

1. _____
   _____
   _____ (2)

2. _____
   _____ (2)

3. _____
   _____ (2)

4. _____
   _____ (2)

5. _____
   _____ (2)

6. _____
   _____ (2)

7. _____
   _____ (2)

8. _____
   _____ (2)

9. _____
   _____ (2)

10. _____
    _____ (2)

Commas for lists

Commas can be used within sentences – between the opening capital letter and the concluding full stop – to separate items in a list.

The punctuation pattern looks something like this:

A , , , and/or .

For example:

> We packed the picnic basket with sandwiches, fruit, bottled water and wet wipes.
>
> When they saw the sea the children hurried, scurried, frolicked and tumbled across the beach to get to it.
>
> In Kipling's famous story, the elephant's child found the great, grey-green, greasy Limpopo River.
>
> They crept forward slowly, cautiously, quietly and in terror.
>
> We are looking for actors, dancers, singers or strong all-round performers.

Notice two things:

- Word lists separated by commas can be nouns, verbs, adjectives or adverbs.
- You do *not* need a comma after the last item in the list or before 'and' (or sometimes 'or').

> Addresses on envelopes are usually now written without punctuation.

> Always remember that the purpose of punctuation is to make meaning clearer. For example, 'I like cooking my cat and my family' means something rather different from 'I like cooking, my cat and my family'.

Exercise

Create eight sentences on the opposite page. Each sentence should contain a list of words separated by commas – two each for nouns, verbs, adjectives and adverbs.

1 _____
  _____
  _____
  _____ (2)

2 _____
  _____
  _____
  _____ (2)

3 _____
  _____
  _____
  _____ (2)

4 _____
  _____
  _____
  _____ (2)

5 _____
  _____
  _____
  _____ (2)

6 _____
  _____
  _____
  _____ (2)

7 _____
  _____
  _____
  _____ (2)

8 _____
  _____
  _____
  _____ (2)

Commas for lists

Semicolons for lists

Sometimes a list gets complex. Instead of consisting of single items, it includes additional information about each item.

You might write the following sentence that uses commas:

> I went to the supermarket and bought oranges, bananas, pears and cherries.

If, on the other hand, you want to write a more complex list, you will need commas within each item:

> I went the supermarket and bought:
>
> ... oranges, Granny's favourite
>
> ... bananas because Paul, Rosie and I all like them with ice cream
>
> ... pears, several varieties, which all work well in smoothies
>
> ... and freshly picked cherries, succulent and shiny as they lay in their box.

In this case, you should use semicolons to separate the items:

> I went to the supermarket and bought oranges, Granny's favourite; bananas because Paul, Rosie and I all like them with ice cream; pears, several varieties, which all work well in smoothies and freshly picked cherries, succulent and shiny as they lay in their box.

Note that you don't need a semicolon with the 'and' that comes before the final item ('freshly picked cherries').

Note too that you do not need a capital letter after a semicolon – other than for a proper noun – because you are in the middle of a sentence.

> Semi-colons used to be used a great deal. See the writing of Charles Dickens or Jane Austen, for example. Over the years, semi-colons have gradually disappeared. Apart from, very occasionally, in a complex list, it is probably better not to use them. Good writers now use less punctuation than their predecessors did.

Exercise

1 Punctuate this sentence with commas and semicolons.

There were white-tusked old males with fallen leaves and nuts and twigs lying in the wrinkles of their necks and the folds of their ears fat slow-footed she-elephants with restless little pinky black calves only three or four feet high running under their stomachs young elephants with their tusks just beginning to show and very proud of them lanky scraggy old female elephants savage old bull elephants and there was one with a broken tusk and the marks of the full-stroke the terrible drawing scrape of a tiger's claws on his side. (7)

Adapted from *The Jungle Book* by Rudyard Kipling (1894)

2 Write two long sentences of your own using semicolons to divide a complex list.

(a) _____ (2)

(b) _____ (2)

Collective nouns

Collective nouns are words used for a group or set of something:

> **pack** of cards
>
> **pod** of whales
>
> **orchestra** (of players)
>
> **gang** of thieves

A collective noun is singular, so:

> The orchestra played under **its** conductor at Fairfield Halls.
>
> Farmer Smith has a flock of sheep which **grazes** in his paddock.

Of course, if there is more than one of the collective noun, it is plural:

> We heard three different orchestras under **their** various conductors at Fairfield Halls.
>
> Last week Farmer Smith bought Farmer Wright's flock so now two flocks **graze** in his paddock.

> *'Two' means 2. 'Too' means too much of something. (We were too full to eat pudding.) Or it means in addition to. (I think so too.) Use 'to' in every other case.*

> *Lovely is an adjective, not an adverb. 'That's a lovely dress.' 'Her singing is lovely.' (Not, 'She sings lovely'.)*

Exercise

1 Draw lines to link each of the following collective nouns with what it refers to.

division	beavers
cete	geese
company	lions
pride	witches
quiver	ships
colony	soldiers
parliament	badgers
fleet	actors
coven	owls
gaggle	arrows (10)

2 Use each of the collective nouns above in a sentence of your own. Use some of them as plurals.

(a) _____
_____ (2)

(b) _____
_____ (2)

(c) _____
_____ (2)

(d) _____
_____ (2)

(e) _____
_____ (2)

(f) _____
_____ (2)

(g) _____
_____ (2)

(h) _____
_____ (2)

(i) _____
_____ (2)

(j) _____
_____ (2)

Verb tenses

All verbs are expressed in one of three tenses:

> Present tense: She walks.
>
> Past tense: She walked.
>
> Future tense: She will walk.

Each of these comes in various forms with different meanings. For example:

> She is walking.
>
> She was walking. She has walked. She had been walking. She has been walking.
>
> She will have walked. She will have been walking. She will be walking.

Tenses are concerned with time.

Every verb indicates either that something is happening now (present tense), at some point in the past (past tense) or some time in the future (future tense).

> 'Past' is a noun, adverb, adjective or preposition. (Let's consider the past. Past times are interesting. The soldiers marched past the statue.) 'Passed' is the past tense of the verb 'to pass'. (We passed the motorway service station.)

> *Like* is a verb meaning to favour ('I like ice cream') or a slippery word, sometimes a conjunction, sometimes a preposition and sometimes an adverb relating to comparison ('I am like my dad'). Don't use it in any other way!

Exercise

1 Write three sentences using verbs in the past tense starting with:

(a) Yesterday _____

_____

_____ (2)

(b) Last week _____

_____

_____ (2)

(c) When I was a baby _____

_____

_____ (2)

2 Write three sentences in the present tense starting with:

(a) At the moment _____

_____

_____ (2)

(b) When we are at home _____

_____

_____ (2)

(c) Today _____

_____

_____ (2)

3 Write three sentences in the future tense starting with:

(a) Tomorrow _____

_____

_____ (2)

(b) When we reach Scotland _____

_____

_____ (2)

(c) Next year _____

_____

_____ (2)

Compound nouns

These are single nouns made up of two or more words linked together.

> They can be:
> - formed of words with spaces between them (washing machine, swimming pool)
> - separated by hyphens (sister-in-law, no-man's-land)
> - formed of words that have joined together to create new words (footnote, grasshopper).
>
> In some cases you can choose which of these you use. Air stream, air-stream and airstream are all allowed by dictionaries. In other cases you simply have to learn which is right. For example, greatuncle would definitely be wrong, as would fishing-rod.

> A greenhouse is a glass building in which plants are grown. A green house is a house that is painted green. Take care with compound words.

> Habits and rules gradually change. You might see, for example, hyphens in compound nouns in old books where we wouldn't now use them. Walking stick, for example, no longer needs a hyphen. Neither does pineapple. In the time of Charles Dickens both words took a hyphen.

> Sentences can, and should, start with different parts of speech. For example:
> - Sometimes we walk home. (adverb)
> - Young children are welcome. (adjective)
> - Sit up straight. (verb)
> - On the bus were three passengers. (preposition)
> - Because of the rain we took shelter. (conjunction)
> - Tigers are an endangered species. (noun)

Answers

Conjunctions (page 5)

Exercise
These are example answers:
1. You should eat green vegetables <u>so</u> you'll be healthy.
   You should eat green vegetables <u>and</u> you'll be healthy.
   Eating green vegetables will make you healthy.
2. She worked hard <u>although</u> she was badly paid.
   She worked hard <u>but</u> she was badly paid.
   Despite working hard, she was not paid well.
3. In Britain you have to be 17 to drive a car <u>whereas</u> in parts of America you can start at 15.
   In Britain you have to be 17 to drive a car <u>but</u> in parts of America you can start at 15.
   In parts of America you can start to drive at 15, which is different from Britain where you can't start until you are 17.
4. He says he dislikes reading <u>yet</u> he does a lot of it.
   He says he dislikes reading <u>unless</u> he does a lot of it.
   He only enjoys reading if he does a lot of it.
5. Please visit us <u>and</u> we'll show you the local sights.
   Please visit us <u>because</u> we'll show you the local sights.
   If you come to visit us we'll show you the local sights.
6. Ask <u>and</u> you will receive.
   Ask <u>so</u> you will receive.
   Ask in order that you receive.
7. I like all the swimming instructors at the club <u>but</u> Mr Jackson is my favourite.
   I like all the swimming instructors at the club <u>although</u> Mr Jackson is my favourite.
   Despite the fact that Mr Jackson is my favourite swimming instructor at the club, I like all the others too.
8. Come over here <u>so</u> you can see the view from this window.
   Come over here <u>for</u> you can see the view from this window.
   Come over to the window because you see the view from there.
9. I shall choose a book by Michael Morpurgo <u>or</u> Theresa Breslin.
   I shall choose a book by Michael Morpurgo <u>and</u> Theresa Breslin.
   I am going to choose a book that is written by both authors.
10. 'Sit down and listen,' Mrs Summers <u>or</u> Mrs Erskine would say to us.
    'Sit down and listen,' Mrs Summers <u>and</u> Mrs Erskine would say to us.
    Both Mrs Summers and Mrs Erskine would say to us, 'Sit down and listen.'

Nouns (page 9)

Exercise
1. <u>Girls</u> and <u>boys</u> usually like learning <u>history</u>. (common, common, abstract)
2. On the <u>way</u> to <u>Weymouth</u>, <u>Uncle Jake</u> and I saw a <u>lark</u> and a <u>charm</u> of <u>goldfinches</u>. (abstract, proper, proper (Uncle Jake), common, collective, common)
3. <u>Brighton</u> and <u>Eastbourne</u> are <u>towns</u> on the south <u>coast</u> of <u>England</u>. (proper, proper, common, common, proper)
4. <u>Mrs Peters</u> spoke to each <u>player</u> in the <u>team</u>. (proper, common, collective)
5. <u>Guy Fawkes</u> was found guilty of <u>treason</u>. (proper, abstract)
6. <u>Maria Jensen</u> has a <u>passion</u> for classical <u>music</u>. (proper, abstract, abstract)
7. <u>Theft</u> is illegal in every <u>culture</u>. (abstract, abstract)
8. <u>Questions</u> and <u>answers</u> are welcome in all our <u>lessons</u>. (abstract, abstract, abstract)
9. Did <u>Jane Austen</u> live in <u>Hampshire</u>? (proper, proper)
10. <u>Buckingham Palace</u> is the main <u>place</u> of <u>residence</u> of <u>Her Majesty the Queen</u>. (proper, common, abstract, proper)

Verbs (page 10)

Exercise 1
These are example answers:
1. scampered, hurtled, dashed, hurried, raced, jogged, sprinted
2. demanded, wondered, questioned, requested, begged, interrogated, beseeched
3. reclined, rested, squatted, settled, perched

Exercise 2
These are example answers:
1. cried, smiled, laughed
   sat, crouched, stood
2. begun
   finished
3. shone, walked
   beckoned, drove
4. felt, did
   was, was
5. Listen, tell
   Watch, show
6. is, is
   was, was

English Workbook: Grammar and Punctuation Age 9–11 published by Galore Park

Adjectives (page 12)

Exercise 1
These are example answers:
American, Continental, Finnish, Italian, European, Japanese, Victorian, Elizabethan, Liverpudlian, Dickensian, Russian, Churchillian, Kentish, Parisian, Swiss, Brazilian, Georgian, Irish, Mozartian, Glaswegian

Exercise 2
The words in brackets are example answers:
1 <u>Most</u> cattle in Britain are <u>black</u> and <u>white</u> or <u>brown</u>. (few, cream, grey, spotted)
2 I shall ask <u>helpful</u> Mrs Smith or <u>sarcastic</u> Mr Fletcher. (frightening, sympathetic)
3 Shall we go to the <u>shopping</u> centre or the <u>local</u> shops? (leisure, big)
4 My father is a <u>Newcastle</u> boy but my mother is <u>Liverpudlian</u>. (Edinburgh, Glaswegian)
5 You are <u>late</u>. (wrong)
6 <u>Italian</u> cooking beats <u>English</u> or <u>German</u> offerings. (Restaurant, home, school)
7 The <u>centenarian</u> grandmother was <u>alert</u>. (white-haired, tired)
8 <u>Good</u> manners make <u>happy</u> teachers. (thoughtful, cheerful)

Adverbs (page 15)

Exercise
1 These are example answers:
  a now, carefully
  b astonishingly
  c often, impressively
  d energetically, rarely
  e soon, happily
  f often, always
  g really
  h carefully, exactly
2 No answers applicable

What exactly is a sentence? (page 17)

Exercise
These are example answers:
1 Did Ollie, always a sensible boy, agree?
2 Chloe, who was upset about the netball match, cried.
3 The school, whose heating has broken down, is closed.
4 Jamila, my next door neighbour, might know.
5 My train, which is supposed to get me to Manchester by 6 p.m., is late.
6 Has Panjit, such a bookworm, read it?
7 Even Tola, often hard to please, liked it.
8 Felix, getting very cross, stood up.
9 Wait, please, for Emily.
10 Water, at least in most of Europe, is plentiful.

Changing the word order (page 18)

Exercise
These are example answers:
1 Always a sensible boy, did Ollie agree?
2 Upset about the netball match, Chloe cried.
3 With the heating broken down, the school is closed.
4 My next door neighbour, Jamila, might know.
5 Although it is supposed to get me to Manchester by 6 p.m., my train is late.
6 As he's such a bookworm, has Panjit read it?
7 Although she's often hard to please, even Tola liked it.
8 Getting very cross, Felix stood up.
9 Wait for Emily, please.
10 At least in most of Europe, water is plentiful.

Commas for lists (page 20)

Exercise
These are example answers:
1 Nouns:
  (a) For breakfast I like muesli, fruit, croissants or rolls.
  (b) My aunt, uncle, grandmother and three cousins are all coming to stay for the weekend.
2 Verbs:
  (a) I arrived, unpacked, washed and went downstairs.
  (b) Should we go, stay, ring for help or do nothing?
3 Adjectives:
  (a) Who's afraid of the hungry, big, bad wolf?
  (b) That house is cold, draughty, uncomfortable and ugly.
4 Adverbs:
  (a) Let's discuss the matter calmly, logically, quietly and sensibly.
  (b) I wish I could knit neatly, evenly and confidently as my great-aunt does.

Semicolons for lists (page 23)

Exercise
1 There were white-tusked old males, with fallen leaves and nuts and twigs lying in the wrinkles of their necks and the folds of their ears; fat, slow-footed she-elephants with restless, little pinky black calves, only three or four feet high, running under their stomachs; young elephants with their tusks just beginning to show and very proud of them; lanky, scraggy old female elephants; savage old bull elephants and there was one with a broken tusk and the marks of the full-stroke, the terrible drawing scrape of a tiger's claws, on his side.
2 This is an example answer:
I am taught by Mrs Ericson, who is strict but has a good sense of humour; by lively, energetic, enthusiastic Miss Hodges; by Mr Grady, who lives just round the corner from my uncle and aunt and by Old Mr Sullivan, whom everyone's been expecting to retire each year ever since my mum was a pupil at the school.

Collective nouns (page 24)

Exercise

1. division/soldiers, cete/badgers, company/actors, pride/lions, quiver/arrows, colony/beavers, parliament/owls, fleet/ships, coven/witches, gaggle/geese
2. These are example answers:
   (a) At the end of his leave Freddy rejoined his division which was headed for a war zone.
   (b) We love to watch our local cete of badgers at night under ultra-violet lamps.
   (c) There were five actors in the company.
   (d) The guide drove us in the jeep to the spot where he knew we'd be able to see a pride of lions.
   (e) The archers all drew arrows from their quivers and loosed them at the target.
   (f) There were three separate beaver colonies all chewing at the trees on the lake we visited in Canada.
   (g) Parliaments of owls are quite rare in cities but common in the country.
   (h) The three fleets sailed towards each other to form one large one.
   (i) Covens are rare now but were, we're told, common in the Middle Ages.
   (j) Geese are useful guard animals, which is why my grandparents have a gaggle in their garden.

Verb tenses (page 26)

Exercise

These are example answers:

1. (a) Yesterday my neighbour died.
   (b) Last week we were walking along the beach when we unexpectedly met Mr Jones.
   (c) When I was a baby my parents were still living abroad.
2. (a) At the moment I'm reading *Emma* by Jane Austen.
   (b) When we are at home we usually eat dinner together and then disperse to different parts of the house.
   (c) Today is my grandmother's sixtieth birthday.
3. (a) Tomorrow my brother will start at his new school.
   (b) When we reach Scotland my dad will put on his kilt.
   (c) Next year will be the centenary of the founding of our school.

Compound nouns (page 29)

Exercise

1. bookworm
2. buttercup
3. pencil case
4. bagpipes
5. bus stop
6. father-in-law
7. lighthouse
8. frying pan
9. keyboard
10. merry-go-round

Abstract nouns (page 31)

Exercise

These are example answers:

1. (a) If you want your homework to look nice as well as be correct then focus on neatness.
   (b) I wanted to be a prefect but my application was rejected.
   (c) Greatness is a very rare quality although some say that Nelson Mandela had it.
   (d) We answered all the police officer's questions and were thanked for our helpfulness.
   (e) It is my sister's ambition to be an airline pilot.
   (f) The fusion of gasses can lead to dramatic results.
2. (a) education
   (b) readiness
   (c) awkwardness
   (d) perspiration
   (e) production
   (f) weakness
   (g) explosion
   (g) happiness
   (h) dictation
   (i) saltiness

English Workbook: Grammar and Punctuation Age 9–11 published by Galore Park

A3

Colons (page 32)

Exercise
1 As Shakespeare said: a rose by any other name would smell as sweet.
2 As the train heads towards Scotland look out for the following: the Angel of the North, Durham cathedral and the north west coastline.
3 We'd like written opinions on this matter from: boys, girls, teachers, other staff, parents and anyone else who is interested.
4 We were told we were to read two books in school that term: *Tom's Midnight Garden* and *Oliver Twist*.
5 My sister is taking A levels in four subjects: physics, chemistry, biology and English.
6 The voice of the presenter rang out: 'And here at last is the moment you've been waiting for.'
7 There are two periods in life when you need care and help: when it is beginning and when it is drawing to a close.
8 The buses arrived at the times stated in the timetable: 4.45 and 5.15.

Gerunds (page 33)

Exercise
These are example answers:
1 Running, Swimming, Rowing
2 singing, dancing, performing
3 writing, cooking, planning
4 driving, cycling
5 liking
6 parachuting, shopping, sunbathing
7 concentrating, relaxing, diving
8 Ironing, decorating

Prepositions (page 34)

Exercise 1
These are example answers:
1 We picnicked below the hilltop.
2 His grandparents live outside Cirencester.
3 At the beach I noticed a lot of debris.
4 We usually take our holidays within Europe.
5 The grass verges near motorways house a lot of wildlife.
6 Was Melissa at PE today?
7 My father is strongly against hunting.
8 They stood before the door.
9 We all ran into the building.
10 Put your bags under the table please.

Exercise 2
These are example answers:
1 During the afternoon we heard helicopters.
2 The cat hid under the table.
3 All litter should go in the bin.
4 We rested the wreath against the war memorial.
5 Did you get those jeans from that shop on the High Street?
6 The village is near the motorway.

Speech marks (page 37)

Exercise 1
1 'The policemen,' said the old lady, 'look younger every day.'
2 'What are you waiting for?' asked Mrs Temple.
3 Miss Lloyd said, 'I'm going to read you a story now.'
4 'Have you seen today's *Guardian*?' asked my uncle.
5 'Get inside quickly!' shouted Dad as it began to snow.
6 'I think you'll enjoy this writing assignment,' said our English teacher, 'and then we'll move on to reading another play in class.'
7 Julius Caesar wrote, 'I came, I saw, I conquered,' but it was Horatius who said, 'Seize the day.'
8 'Ask me if you don't understand,' Miss Dunmore always says in maths.
9 'What are you waiting for?' demanded Ali.
10 'I've often wondered,' my friend said, 'why you always walk so fast.'

Exercise 2
These are example answers:
1 "That's enough," said the Prime Minister.
2 My mum often says, 'You'll feel better after a good sleep'.
3 "Sit down and listen carefully," said Miss Paterson, "I'm going to explain something important."
4 'Macbeth hath murdered sleep' is a quotation from a famous play.
5 Why does he keep shouting, "Down with denim clothes"?

Apostrophes for omission (page 39)

Exercise
1 <u>Let's</u> go and see who won the tennis match.
2 It <u>isn't</u> a good idea to walk outdoors with bare feet.
3 <u>We're</u> expecting my aunt and uncle to arrive at about <u>four o'clock</u>.
4 Surely <u>they're</u> both older than us?
5 We were told that we <u>shouldn't</u> walk along that lonely footpath by ourselves.
6 If you <u>don't</u> know the answer to a question <u>it's</u> best not to waste class time by putting your hand up.
7 <u>Won't</u> you stay and watch TV with us?
8 Our neighbours <u>aren't</u> in and <u>won't</u> be back until about <u>ten o'clock</u> so we <u>don't</u> have to worry too much about the noise.

Parenthesis (page 40)

Exercise
These are example answers:

1 We ran, never our preferred option, as fast as we could to the shops.
2 I have always preferred dogs – so much more friendly – to cats.
3 Home-made bread (especially my grandpa's) beats anything you can buy in a shop.
4 We spend nearly a fifth of the school week doing maths (which I hate) and another fifth on English.
5 Shall I make – or at least reheat – some coffee for Dad?
6 I hope I shan't get behind – or not much, anyway – in science this term.
7 What sort (or style, genre or type) of music do you like?
8 Lee and Lucas, always active, were planning a day's cycling.

Apostrophes for possession (page 43)

Exercise 1

1 Rosie's mother collects her from school by car.
2 The princess's arrival was a great excitement.
3 The princesses' car turned the corner and we could see they were both in the back.
4 Alfie's answers are often wrong.
5 Has Josh's parcel arrived?
6 The twins' christening took place in St Agnes's Church.
7 Mrs Jones's handwriting is very neat.
8 The children's lunch usually starts at noon and the teachers have theirs half an hour later.
9 Players' kit is laundered in the school's own washing machine, which saves families a lot of work.
10 Jess's and Thomas's grandparents' house is like Aladdin's cave.

Exercise 2
These are example answers:

1 Our car's air conditioning is very efficient.
2 Are you in Mr Watts's class this year?
3 The triplets' birth took place in St James's hospital.
4 Men's clothes are often easier to wash than women's garments.
5 All six actresses' dressing rooms were on the same corridor.
6 Did you borrow Mia's book?

Fun with phrasal verbs (page 44)

Exercise
These are example answers:

1 A huge number of people turned out to hear the brass band.
2 After much thought, my dad turned down the job offer.
Hotel chambermaids often turn down their customers' beds in the early evening.
3 'Time to turn in,' said Mum, yawning.
I was surprised that Mrs Smith turned in her own son when she realised he had been stealing.
4 If a prime minister stands down, his deputy takes over until other arrangements can be made.
5 Can you stand in as wicket keeper today because I'm one player short?
6 You have won the competition because your entry really stood out.
7 Casually rolling in to lessons late is not tolerated in our school.
8 We were amazed when the film star rolled up at our house.
9 You cannot change school uniform all at once; it has to be rolled out over several years.
10 Let's roll along to the bakers and see if there are any buns left.
11 She set out at 9 a.m. but didn't arrive until late afternoon.
12 Mr Newington set up a system in the classroom so that we could all see exactly what we had to do next.
13 Tomorrow's football match has been called off.
14 We could call in on Granny.
Because the goods were faulty, the supermarket called in every washing machine it had sold that week.
15 In 1941 my great grandfather was called up to fight in the Second World War.

Flexible words (page 47)

<u>Exercise</u>
These are example answers:

1. I'm just tired. (adverb)
   I thought that was a just decision. (adjective)
2. She ran fast. (adverb)
   She is a fast runner. (adjective)
   Muslims fast during the month of Ramadan. (verb)
   Ramadan is an annual Muslim fast. (noun)
3. 'Are we going to near land before nightfall?' she asked one of the ship's staff. (verb)
   She sits near him in class. (preposition)
   Near neighbours can be a problem if they're noisy. (adjective)
4. Drop scones are my mother's speciality. (adjective)
   Can you drop me at the supermarket? (verb)
   I like just a drop of milk in my tea. (noun)
5. We were surprised by the open door. (adjective)
   Open that door, please. (verb)
6. Game, set and match were won by the reigning champion. (noun)
   In our school they set us by ability in all the main subjects. (verb)
   I prefer set yoghurt to stirred. (adjective)
7. I help to ring the birds in the sanctuary so that we can trace their movements. (verb)
   I inherited this silver ring from my great grandmother. (noun)
   A wedding band is usually worn on the ring finger. (adjective)
8. We need to book those theatre tickets. (verb)
   I left my book on the train. (noun)
   I seem to need a larger book bag for school each year. (adjective)

Adjectives with hyphens (page 50)

<u>Exercise</u>
These are example answers:

1. (a) My uncle has worked in most of the English-speaking world.
   (b) My accident-prone sister has just broken her arm for the third time.
   (c) Sugar-free drinks are a sensible part of healthy living.
   (d) I need an up-to-date list of postage rates.
   (e) We have good facilities for computer-aided design at school.
2. (a) He is just the sort of quick-thinking person you need with you in an emergency.
   Quick thinking is not my strength.
   (b) My sport-mad sister plays three different games on Saturdays.
   I loathe sport, mad as that sounds.
   (c) There are no late-night trains to London.
   That's the late night train.
   (d) I admire his life-like drawing.
   I wish I had a life like hers.

Transitive verbs (page 52)

<u>Exercise</u>
These are example answers:

1. Have you opened that tin yet? (transitive)
   The new library opens on Tuesday. (intransitive)
2. In *Peter Pan* Captain Hook is keen on making people walk the plank. (transitive)
   We'll walk because it's quicker than the bus at this time of day. (intransitive)
3. People who eat shellfish are often ill. (transitive)
   Let's eat before the TV programme starts. (intransitive)
4. My sister begins a new book several times a week. (transitive)
   What time does the film begin? (intransitive)
5. I usually play Scrabble with my Granny. (transitive)
   The band has been playing for an hour. (intransitive)
6. My great granddad flew Spitfires in the Second World War. (transitive)
   Time flies. (intransitive)

Punctuation practice (page 54)

<u>Exercise 1</u>
This is an example answer:

Many families go on holidays in the summer break. Because of this, travel agents, very unfairly, put prices up at peak times. In the past, parents have been permitted to take children away during term time to get round this problem. Was that a good idea? David Cameron's government thought not and changed the law. Do we need more easy-to-access holiday opportunities? If you have a view please sent it to: Esther Peters at Southern TV.

Exercise 2

1. Maria, Bella, Lola and Ruby were waiting for us at Tesco with Bella's mother.
2. When you've finished your French homework it might be a good idea to have some supper before your brothers' arrival because they'll eat everything in sight.
3. 'Help!' cried the distressed Petra Irwin when she realised her dog, Fred, had slithered down the bank into the Mersey.
4. Doctor Patel, who's taught us science for three years, is leaving at Easter to become headmaster of Richfield College Academy.
5. 'I want to get to the shops before they close,' said Aunt Jane, 'because otherwise there'll be nothing for breakfast in the morning.'
6. Finding hard-to-get items is much easier if you Google them rather than going to shops.
7. When my sister, Jemma, married Paul last year she acquired three brothers-in-law: James, Andrew and Duncan.
8. Anne Fine's new book, which comes out in October, could be her best yet.
9. Wouldn't you prefer to stay overnight because you will already have travelled a long way, worked hard and stayed up for a long time?
10. There were tiny, newborn kittens blindly mewing and scrabbling; elderly tomcats with battered faces and tattered ears; sleek, teenage cats, proudly washing themselves, staring arrogantly at visitors and occasionally stretching; tired beasts curled up asleep in the sunshine and taking no notice of anyone and Helga, the exquisite tabby and ginger female we eventually told Mrs Merryman of Battersea Cats that we'd like to offer a home to.

Exercise

Write the correct form of the compound nouns that fit these definitions. Use a dictionary to help you if you need to.

1 compulsive reader
_____ (1)

2 yellow meadow flower
_____ (1)

3 pouch for storing writing tools in
_____ (1)

4 Scottish musical instrument
_____ (1)

5 where you wait for a large public transport vehicle in the street
_____ (1)

6 husband or wife's male parent
_____ (1)

7 flashing tower on coast warning ships at sea
_____ (1)

8 stove-top vessel for cooking eggs and bacon in
_____ (1)

9 set of buttons with letters and numbers to press
_____ (1)

10 old-fashioned word for a funfair roundabout
_____ (1)

All right is two words. So are *thank you* and *a lot*. Do not be tempted to write them incorrectly as many people do.

Abstract nouns

Abstract nouns are often formed by adding a suffix to another word. Here are two examples:

- The suffix **-ness** can be added to an adjective to form an abstract noun:

tired + ness = tiredness

close + ness = closeness

- Note that if the adjective ends in **y** than it changes to an **i** before **-ness**.

silly + ness = silliness

weary + ness = weariness

- Other abstract nouns are formed by the suffix **-ion**, which is usually added to a verb, often with a slight spelling change:

revise + ion = revision (drop the final e)

adore + ion = adoration (drop the final e)

suck + ion = suction (change k to t)

absorb + ion = absorption (change b to p)

The abstract noun formed from the adjective jolly is jollity. It doesn't take -ness like hilly (hilliness) or pally (palliness).

When you use a verb's infinitive (I love *to swim*/I'd prefer *to be* at home), try not to break it up with other words such as adverbs. Write, for example: 'I love to swim often' or 'I often love to swim' rather than 'I love to often swim'. 'Split infinitives' can be very awkward and inelegant.

Exercise

1 Use the following abstract nouns in sentences of your own.

(a) neatness

_____

_____ (2)

(b) application

_____

_____ (2)

(c) greatness

_____

_____ (2)

(d) helpfulness

_____

_____ (2)

(e) ambition

_____

_____ (2)

(f) fusion

_____

_____ (2)

2 Use **-ness** or **-ion** to form abstract nouns from these words, changing the spelling where necessary. Use a dictionary to help you if you need to.

(a) educate _____ (1)   **(b)** ready _____ (1)

(c) awkward _____ (1)   **(d)** perspire _____ (1)

(e) produce _____ (1)   **(f)** weak _____ (1)

(g) explode _____ (1)   **(h)** happy _____ (1)

(i) dictate _____ (1)   **(j)** salty _____ (1)

Colons

A colon (:) means 'like this' or 'as follows'. Use it to introduce a list or, sometimes, words spoken.

> The following people were present: the chairman of governors, the principal and several teachers.
>
> This is what she said: 'No, I won't!'

It is also often used in notes, letters and instructions. I often use it in this book before an example, for instance:

> Send your competition entries to: Mrs P Hartley, 24 Oak Road, PL12 8HJ.
>
> Colours of the spectrum: red, orange, yellow, green, blue, indigo, violet.

> Use 'can' and 'may' accurately. 'Can' means an ability to do something. 'May' implies permission. You *can* go to the toilet (obviously!); the question is *may* you go to the toilet.

Exercise

Add colons to the following. All the other punctuation has been done for you.

1. As Shakespeare said a rose by any other name would smell as sweet. (1)
2. As the train heads towards Scotland look out for the following the Angel of the North, Durham cathedral and the north west coastline. (1)
3. We'd like written opinions on this matter from boys, girls, teachers, other staff, parents and anyone else who is interested. (1)
4. We were told we were to read two books in school that term *Tom's Midnight Garden and Oliver Twist*. (1)
5. My sister is taking A levels in four subjects physics, chemistry, biology and English. (1)
6. The voice of the presenter rang out 'And here, at last, is the moment you've been waiting for.' (1)
7. There are two periods in life when you need care and help when it is beginning and when it is drawing to a close. (1)
8. The buses arrived at the times stated in the timetable 4.45 and 5.15. (1)

Gerunds

Gerunds are nouns formed by adding the suffix **-ing** to a verb. They are all abstract nouns. Think of them as verbal nouns if it helps.

> talk + ing = talking
>
> Talking is not allowed in exams.
>
> hear + ing = hearing
>
> Hearing is a very important sense.

As with other suffixes, the spelling of the base word sometimes changes when the suffix is added.

> spin + ing = spinning (add an extra n)
>
> Spinning is an old craft.
>
> pot + ing = potting (add an extra t)
>
> My granny's favourite garden activity is potting.

A gerund – or verbal noun – ends in -ing. Note though that not all -ing words are gerunds.

Exercise

Add suitable gerunds to these sentences. Remember that gerunds always end in **-ing**.

1 _____ is my favourite form of exercise. (1)

2 My brother loves _____ but I prefer _____, although we both like _____. (1)

3 Have you finished your _____? (1)

4 We are planning to include both _____ and _____ during this year's holiday. (1)

5 Given his _____ for cats it's no surprise that my uncle has four. (1)

6 I have never understood why people enjoy _____. (1)

7 I am not good at _____. (1)

8 _____ is my dad's job but my mum does all the _____. (1)

Prepositions

Prepositions are useful little words that tell you where something is in relation to something else.

> The book was **on** (or: **under**, **near**, **by**) the table.
>
> We walked **along** (or: **below**, **above**, **around**) the path.
>
> Other prepositions include: inside, outside, at, in, about, before, against, across, behind, beneath, into, without, beside and round.

Be aware though that many of these words are good multi-taskers. They can do more than one job and they aren't always prepositions. You have to look at how they're used to work out which job they're doing.

*Remember that a pre*position *often tells you the position of something.*

Exercise 1

Change each of the prepositions in these sentences to a different one. This may alter the meaning of the sentence. For example: 'The hamster is **in** the cage' could be changed to 'The hamster is **beside** the cage.'

1 We picnicked near the hilltop.

_____

_____ (2)

2 His grandparents live in Cirencester.

_____

_____ (2)

3 Along the beach I noticed a lot of debris.

_____

_____ (2)

4 We usually take our holidays outside Europe.

_____

_____ (2)

5 The grass verges alongside motorways house a lot of wildlife.

_____

_____ (2)

6 Was Melissa in PE today?

_____

_____ (2)

7 My father is strongly into hunting.

_____

_____ (2)

8 They stood behind the door.

_____

_____ (2)

9 We all ran round the building.

_____

_____ (2)

10 Put your bags on the table please.

_____

_____ (2)

Exercise 2

Write six sentences of your own using prepositions. Underline the prepositions you have used.'

1 _____ (2)

2 _____ (2)

3 _____ (2)

4 _____ (2)

5 _____ (2)

6 _____ (2)

Speech marks

If you're writing fiction you usually need to tell your reader which of your characters has said what. You also need to do this if, for example, you are reporting a piece of news and wish to quote someone.

The exact words that someone has spoken need to be enclosed in speech marks – also called inverted commas, quotation marks or quotes. They can be single or double but must be consistent throughout a piece of writing.

> 'Sit down there and wait for the others,' said Mr Ward.
>
> "Sit down there," said Mr Ward.

Words such as 'said Mr Ward' or 'Mr Ward said' can go at the beginning, in the middle or at the end of your sentence.

> Mr Ward said, 'Sit down there and wait for the others'.
>
> "Sit down there," said Mr Ward, "and wait for the others."
>
> 'Sit down there and wait for the others,' Mr Ward said.

> In some countries such as Ireland, some writers use long dashes instead of speech marks to show that a character has begun to speak.

> *Who* is a pronoun used as the subject of a sentence, phrase or clause. 'Who is coming ice skating?' 'I wonder who wrote that?'
>
> Use *whom* when it is not the subject and it is followed by a preposition such as *by, with, from, at, to,* and so on. 'At whom was that missile thrown?' 'With whom did you see that film?'

Exercise 1

Add inverted commas to these sentences. All the other punctuation has been added for you.

1 The policemen, said the old lady, look younger every day. (2)

2 What are you waiting for? asked Mrs Temple. (2)

3 Miss Lloyd said I'm going to read you a story now. (2)

4 Have you seen today's *Guardian*? asked my uncle. (2)

5 Get inside quickly! shouted Dad as it began to snow. (2)

6 I think you'll enjoy this writing assignment, said our English teacher, and then we'll move on to reading another play in class. (2)

7 Julius Caesar wrote, I came, I saw, I conquered, but it was Horatius who said, Seize the day. (2)

8 Ask me if you don't understand, Miss Dunmore always says in maths. (2)

9 What are you waiting for? demanded Ali. (2)

10 I've often wondered, my friend said, why you always walk so fast. (2)

Exercise 2

Write five sentences of your own using speech marks. Vary their shape as much as you can. Put the breaks between the words spoken in different places.

1 _____ (2)
2 _____ (2)
3 _____ (2)
4 _____ (2)
5 _____ (2)

Apostrophes for omission

The apostrophe (') has two jobs (see page 42 for the other).

It stands in for a missing letter or letters:

> **Isn't** is short for **is not**.
>
> **O'clock** is short for the old-fashioned expression **of the clock**.
>
> **M'way** on a signpost is short for **motorway**.

It's means *it is* or *it has*. (It's been a lovely day.) If you do not mean *it is* or *it has* you should use *its* (without an apostrophe).

We're means *we are*. *Were* is part of the verb *to be*. (We were ready.)

Shan't is a contraction of *shall not*. Various letters have disappeared but it takes only a single apostrophe.

Their indicates possession. (They won their match). *They're* means *they are*. Use *there* in every other case.

Far more words ending with s do not need an apostrophe than need one. This sentence, for example, needs no apostrophes at all: Mrs Peters likes to stress that all the boys and girls in all Year 6 classes should use the stairs behind the performing arts studios.

Exercise

Write out these sentences adding the shortened form of the words in brackets with the correct apostrophes.

1 **(Let us)** go and see who won the tennis match.

_____ (2)

2 It **(is not)** a good idea to walk outdoors with bare feet.

_____ (2)

3 **(We are)** expecting my aunt and uncle to arrive at about **(four of the clock)**.

_____ (2)

4 Surely **(they are)** both older than us?

_____ (2)

5 We were told that we **(should not)** walk along that lonely footpath by ourselves.

_____ (2)

6 If you **(do not)** know the answer to a question **(it is)** best not to waste class time by putting your hand up.

_____ (2)

7 **(Will not)** you stay and watch TV with us?

_____ (2)

8 Our neighbours **(are not)** in and **(will not)** be back until about **(ten of the clock)** so we **(do not)** have to worry too much about the noise.

_____ (2)

Apostrophes for omission

39

Parenthesis

If a group of words is separated from the rest of the sentence by a pair of commas (see page 16) or a pair of brackets or dashes, it is said to be in parenthesis.

Words in parenthesis usually provide information that is less important than the rest of the sentence. The sentence would still make sense if the parenthesised words were left out.

For example:

> We asked Great Granny, probably for the hundredth time, to tell us about being bombed out of her home in the Second World War.
>
> We asked Great Granny – probably for the hundredth time – to tell us about being bombed out of her home in the Second World War.
>
> We asked Great Granny (probably for the hundredth time) to tell us about being bombed out of her home in the Second World War.

Notice that the five words in parenthesis – however they are punctuated – could be omitted without losing the sense of the sentence.

> *Information within a sentence marked off with a pair of commas is known as a parenthesis. Note that the plural of parenthesis is parentheses.*

Exercise

Write each of these sentences out again, adding words in parenthesis where indicated.

Use commas, brackets or dashes to separate them off and vary which you choose so that you use all three punctuation options in the course of the exercise.

1 We ran *parenthesis* as fast as we could to the shops.

_____

_____

_____ (2)

2 I have always preferred dogs *parenthesis* to cats.
_____
_____
_____ (2)

3 Home-made bread *parenthesis* beats anything you can buy in a shop.
_____
_____
_____ (2)

4 We spend nearly a fifth of the school week doing maths *parenthesis* and another fifth on English.
_____
_____
_____ (2)

5 Shall I make *parenthesis* some coffee for Dad?
_____
_____
_____ (2)

6 I hope I shan't get behind *parenthesis* in science this term.
_____
_____
_____ (2)

7 What sort *parenthesis* of music do you like?
_____
_____
_____ (2)

8 Lee and Lucas *parenthesis* were planning a day's cycling.
_____
_____
_____ (2)

Apostrophes for possession

The apostrophe's second job (see page 38 for the first) is to show possession – that something is in some sense 'owned' by something or someone else.

> John's shoes (shoes that belong to John)
>
> St Mary's church (church of St Mary)
>
> my friend's house (house that my friend lives in)

In each case **s** is added to the possessor or the word doing the possessing.

Even if a word already ends in **s** or **ss** the same rule applies:

> St James's Church
>
> the actress's dress
>
> Ross's mother

If the possessor is plural the apostrophe is added to the **s** that forms the plural:

> three dogs' leads (the leads of three dogs)
>
> the fathers' race (the race to be run by several fathers)
>
> teachers' car park (where several teachers park their cars)

The only exception to this rule is a handful of nouns that do not take an **s** in their plural form. When they become possessive they behave as if they are singular:

> children's party
>
> women's toilet
>
> men's interests

Exercise 1

Add apostrophes as they are needed in the following sentences.

1. Rosies mother collects her from school by car. (1)

2. The princesss arrival was a great excitement. (1)

3. The princesses car turned the corner and we could see they were both in the back. (1)

4. Alfies answers are often wrong. (1)

5. Has Joshs parcel arrived? (1)

6. The twins christening took place in St Agness Church. (1)

7. Mrs Joness handwriting is very neat. (1)

8. The childrens lunch usually starts at noon and the teachers have theirs half an hour later. (1)

9. Players kit is laundered in the schools own washing machine, which saves families a lot of work. (1)

10. Jesss and Thomass grandparents house is like Aladdins cave. (1)

Exercise 2

Write six sentences of your own using apostrophes for possession.

1. _____
   _____ (2)

2. _____
   _____ (2)

3. _____
   _____ (2)

4. _____
   _____ (2)

5. _____
   _____ (2)

6. _____
   _____ (2)

Apostrophes for possession

Fun with phrasal verbs

Phrasal verbs are verbs that have a preposition or adverb attached to them to give them a new meaning. For example:

> Give in (concede)
>
> Turn up (arrive)
>
> Ask out (invite)
>
> Stand over (supervise)

We use phrasal verbs in English all the time in our everyday speech and often they have more than one meaning. They cause people who are learning English a lot of problems.

Think, for example, of the differences in meaning between:

> to run over (to hit a pedestrian with a vehicle)
>
> to run out (to find that you have used up all of something such as milk)
>
> to run up (to incur a lot of expenses and get a big bill)
>
> a run-in (slang for a disagreement with some official, such as the police)

or

> to come in (to enter)
>
> to come over (to visit from some way away)
>
> to come up (to arrive perhaps via stairs or by walking uphill)
>
> to come out (to tell the truth about yourself or something you believe in)

Exercise

Use the phrasal verbs opposite and on the following page in sentences of your own. Remember that each of your sentences needs a capital letter at the beginning and a full stop at the end. You may find you need a comma or a pair of commas inside your sentence.

Change the form of the verb if you wish to use a different person or tense. You could, for example, use turned or turns instead of turn.

1 Turn out

_____
_____
_____ (2)

2 Turn down

_____
_____
_____ (2)

3 Turn in

_____
_____
_____ (2)

4 Stand down

_____
_____
_____ (2)

5 Stand in

_____
_____
_____ (2)

6 Stand out

_____
_____
_____ (2)

7 Roll in

_____
_____
_____ (2)

Fun with phrasal verbs

8 Roll up
_____
_____
_____ (2)

9 Roll out
_____
_____
_____ (2)

10 Roll along
_____
_____
_____ (2)

11 Set out
_____
_____
_____ (2)

12 Set up
_____
_____
_____ (2)

13 Call off
_____
_____
_____ (2)

14 Call in
_____
_____
_____ (2)

15 Call up
_____
_____
_____ (2)

Flexible words

Some words have a range of different meanings and grammatical jobs.

Consider the word 'break':

> Can you **break** that chocolate bar into three even pieces, please? (verb)
>
> My aunts have taken up **break** dancing. (adjective)
>
> We'll chat about it during **break**. (noun)

Or the word 'door':

> The **door** handle is broken and needs replacing. (adjective)
>
> Shut the **door**, if you don't mind. (noun)

Consider words such as 'floor' (I was floored, floor tile, on the floor), 'table' (table an idea, learn a times table, table football) and many other examples.

> 'Beside' means at the side of. (The nurse stood beside the bed.) 'Besides' means in addition to. (Several girls were there besides Emma.)

Exercise

1 Write two sentences using the word 'just' as an adverb and then an adjective.

   (a) _____

   _____ (2)

   (b) _____

   _____ (2)

2 Write four sentences using the word 'fast' as an adverb, an adjective, a verb and then a noun.

(a) _____

_____ (2)

(b) _____

_____ (2)

(c) _____

_____ (2)

(d) _____

_____ (2)

3 Write three sentences using the word 'near' as a verb, a preposition and then an adjective.

(a) _____

_____ (2)

(b) _____

_____ (2)

(c) _____

_____ (2)

4 Write three sentences using the word 'drop' as an adjective, a verb and then a noun.

(a) _____

_____ (2)

(b) _____

_____ (2)

(c) _____

_____ (2)

5 Write two sentences using the word 'open' as an adjective and then a verb.

(a) _____

_____ (2)

(b) _____

_____ (2)

Flexible words

6 Write three sentences using the word 'set' as a noun, a verb and then an adjective.

(a) _____

_____ (2)

(b) _____

_____ (2)

(c) _____

_____ (2)

7 Write three sentences using the word 'ring' as a verb, a noun and then an adjective.

(a) _____

_____ (2)

(b) _____

_____ (2)

(c) _____

_____ (2)

8 Write three sentences using the word 'book' as a verb, a noun and then an adjective.

(a) _____

_____ (2)

(b) _____

_____ (2)

(c) _____

_____ (2)

> The word *set* has more meanings and uses than any other word in English.

> Punctuate for clarity and accuracy but do not clutter your writing with unnecessary punctuation.

Adjectives with hyphens

Some adjectives consist of more than one word or idea so they need hyphens when they come before a noun. These are known as compound adjectives.

For example, when part-time and full-time come before a noun they are hyphenated. So is never-to-be-forgotten.

Hyphens show that the words are linked to form a new one. And they affect meaning.

A heavy metal detector, for example, is a metal detector which is heavy. A heavy-metal detector is a device for detecting heavy metal.

And consider the difference between these two sentences:

> I saw a man-eating tiger.
> I saw a man eating tiger.

Be aware, though, that over time hyphens tend to disappear and words simply join together permanently. Handmade (as in handmade clothes) and tabletop (as in tabletop sale), for example, would probably once have taken a hyphen but no longer do.

> You can use far-too-often-sidelined hyphens to create your own up-to-the-minute adjectives.

Exercise

1 Put these compound adjectives into sentences of your own:

(a) English-speaking

_____

_____ (2)

(b) accident-prone

_____

_____ (2)

(c) sugar-free

_____

_____ (2)

(d) up-to-date

_____

_____ (2)

(e) computer-aided

_____

_____ (2)

2 Write sentences (two for each) to show the difference made by the hyphen. You should be able to have fun with this!

(a) quick-thinking and quick thinking

_____

_____

_____

_____ (4)

(b) sport-mad and sport mad

_____

_____

_____

_____ (4)

(c) late-night and late night

_____

_____

_____

_____ (4)

(d) life-like and life like

_____

_____

_____

_____ (4)

Transitive verbs

Some verbs are transitive. That means that they don't make complete sense without an object to receive the action.

For example:

> She buys apples.

The verb 'buys' cannot (usually) be used without an object – apples in this example.

Here's another:

> I shall attach the document to this email.

The verb 'shall attach' means nothing until the object – 'document' – is added.

Other transitive verbs include: give, get, make, owe, tell, hit, like, mend, repair, build.

There is a slight complication, however.

Many verbs in English can be used both transitively (needing an object) and intransitively (making sense without an object).

For example:

> She dances. (intransitive – meaning that she is fond of dancing and often does it)
>
> She dances a tango. (transitive – the tango is what she dances; grammatically, 'tango' is the object of the verb 'dance')
>
> They've moved. (intransitive – probably meaning they have moved to a different house)
>
> They've moved their goalie. (transitive – probably meaning that they have placed their goalkeeper in a different position and replaced him or her with another player; grammatically, 'goalie' is the object of the verb 'moved')

Exercise

Write two separate sentences using each of the verbs opposite (in any tense you wish). Use each one first as a transitive verb and second as an intransitive verb.

1 open

(a) _____

_____ (2)

(b) _____

_____ (2)

2 walk

(a) _____

_____ (2)

(b) _____

_____ (2)

3 eat

(a) _____

_____ (2)

(b) _____

_____ (2)

4 begin

(a) _____

_____ (2)

(b) _____

_____ (2)

5 play

(a) _____

_____ (2)

(b) _____

_____ (2)

6 fly

(a) _____

_____ (2)

(b) _____

_____ (2)

Transitive verbs

Punctuation practice

Here is an opportunity to practise everything you have learned or revised about punctuation in this workbook.

Remember:

- capital letters
- full stops
- question marks
- hyphens
- commas
- semicolons
- colons
- apostrophes.

> The word 'punctuation' comes from a Latin word meaning 'point'. The full stop is still sometimes called a 'full point' by printers, typesetters, website designers, and so on.

Exercise 1

Write a paragraph using as many punctuation marks as you can. Then swap with a friend and take it in turns to dictate your passages to each other.

_____
_____
_____
_____
_____
_____
_____
_____
_____ (8)

Exercise 2

Punctuate these sentences. You will need to write them out yourself correctly in order to do this properly.

1 maria bella lola and ruby were waiting for us at tesco with bellas mother

(2)

2 when you've finished your french homework it might be a good idea to have some supper before your brothers arrival because theyll eat everything in sight

(2)

3 help cried the distressed petra irwin when she realised her dog fred had slithered down the bank into the mersey

(2)

4 doctor patel whos taught us science for three years is leaving at easter to become headmaster of richfield college academy

(2)

5 i want to get to the shops before they close said aunt jane because otherwise therell be nothing for breakfast in the morning

(2)

6 finding hard to get items is much easier if you google them rather than going to shops

(2)

7 when my sister jemma married paul last year she acquired three brothers in law james andrew and duncan

_____
_____
_____ (2)

8 anne fines new book which comes out in october could be her best yet

_____
_____
_____ (2)

9 wouldnt you prefer to stay overnight because you will already have travelled a long way worked hard and stayed up for a long time

_____
_____
_____ (2)

10 there were tiny newborn kittens blindly mewing and scrabbling elderly tomcats with battered faces and tattered ears sleek teenage cats proudly washing themselves staring arrogantly at visitors and occasionally stretching tired beasts curled up asleep in the sunshine and taking no notice of anyone and helga the exquisite tabby and ginger female we eventually told mrs merryman of battersea cats that we'd like to offer a home to

_____
_____
_____
_____
_____
_____
_____
_____ (2)